AFRICAN-AMERICAN ARTS

COOKING

Angela Shelf Medearis and Michael R. Medearis

Twenty-First Century Books
A Division of Henry Holt and Company • New York

Twenty-First Century Books
A Division of Henry Holt and Company, Inc.
115 West 18th Street
New York, NY 10011

Henry Holt® and colophon are trademarks of
Henry Holt and Company, Inc.
Publishers since 1866

Published in Canada by Fitzhenry & Whiteside Ltd.
195 Allstate Parkway, Markham, Ontario, L3R 4T8

Library of Congress Cataloging-in-Publication Data
Medearis, Angela Shelf, 1956-
Cooking/Angela Shelf Medearis, Michael R. Medearis.
p. cm.—(African-American arts)
Includes bibliographical references (p.) and index.
Summary: Introduces the influence of African-based foods,
cooking techniques, and traditions to American culinary history.
1. Afro-American cookery—History—Juvenile literature. [1. Afro-American cookery—History.
2. Cookery, American] I. Medearis, Michael. II. Title. III. Series.
TX715.M482   1997   97-8071
641.59'296073—DC21   CIP
                                                                 AC
ISBN 0-8050-4484-1
First Edition—1997

DESIGNED BY KELLY SOONG

Printed in the United States of America
All first editions are printed on acid-free paper ∞.

1 3 5 7 9 10 8 6 4 2

Photo credits

p. 4 (top): ©Susan Meiselas/Magnum Photos; p. 4 (bottom): ©Denis Valentine/The Stock Market;
p. 8: ©Burt Glinn/Magnum Photos; p. 9: Vallee des Nobles-Tombe de Nakht, Thebes/Giraudon,
Paris/SuperStock; p. 11: ©Steve McCurry/Magnum Photos; p. 12: © Gerald Buthaud/Cosmos/
Woodfin Camp; p. 13: ©Tim Gibson/ENVISION; p. 15: ©Bruno Barbey/Magnum Photos; pp. 19, 20,
48: ©The Granger Collection; p. 21: ©Dennis Stock/Magnum Photos; p. 23: ©Chris Steele-
Perkins/Magnum Photos; p. 27: ©Allen Lee Page/The Stock Market; p. 30: David David Gallery,
Philadelphia/SuperStock; pp. 35, 41: ©Culver Pictures; p. 37: ©American Stock/Archive Photos; p. 43:
©Solomon D. Butcher Collection/Nebraska State Historical Society; p. 44: ©UPI/Corbis-Bettmann;
p. 45: ©J. B. Marshall/ENVISION; p. 50: Photo courtesy of Griffith Laboratories, Inc., One Griffith
Center, Alsip, IL 60658; p. 53: ©R. Lord/The Image Works; p. 54: ©Goodsmith/The Image Works;
p. 55: ©Betty Press/Woodfin Camp

4-98

SHP

CONTENTS

The heritage continues . . .

INTRODUCTION

When enjoying a steaming serving of seasoned greens, a bowl of spicy gumbo, or a slice of mouth-watering sweet-potato pie, many people are unaware of the African origin of their meal. Most black people were brought to America as slaves from West Africa. While in bondage the captives kept the memories of many of the foods that they had enjoyed in Africa. Okra, sesame seeds, peanuts, and black-eyed peas are just a few of the foods that were grown in Africa and transported to America, often aboard slave ships. Slave cooks knew how to prepare these foods and introduced many new recipes to American cuisine.

African-American food is rich and diverse in taste. And the wonderful smells, flavors, and recipes that have come out of the kitchens of slave cooks remind us of the valuable contributions that African-American chefs have made to the art of cooking.

The variety of foods that were prepared over the years by African-American cooks have greatly influenced a wide range of tastes, from the slave kitchens of the South to the grand, formal dinners of the White House. This book will introduce you to an often unrecognized part of American culinary history—the influence of African-based foods, cooking techniques, and traditions. You will also learn about some of the contributions of individual African Americans to agriculture and food production. The creative impact African-American chefs have had upon food and cooking has spread around the world, but it remains rooted in Africa.

ONE

African Origins of Food and Cooking

African cooking has a long history that can be traced back thousands of years. Many Africans were nomadic people, and the food they ate and the way they prepared it reflected that lifestyle. Since earliest times, fruits and vegetables have been an important part of African cookery. Early African peoples usually did not plant crops but survived by eating the roots, berries, and leaves they gathered. They also fished and hunted and trapped animals for food. Trees and other plants that bore fruit, such as the locust bean, plantain, mango, and papaya, provided a large part of the nomads' diet.

As time went on, only a few peoples lived the nomadic way of life. Others grouped together in villages. Some settled along the African coastline and developed a fishing industry. Cattle, goats, chickens, sheep, ducks, and other farm animals were raised for their milk, blood, and meat. Pork was a rare ingredient in African cooking in any form. Africans of the Muslim faith refused to eat pork, since it was against their religion.

Eventually, more and more Africans cultivated the land and planted crops. Millet was one of the first grains used as food for people and livestock. It was

A typical small village in Guinea

cultivated from a wild weed to the staple crop that we are familiar with today. Millet was popular because it was drought and disease resistant and could grow in different kinds of soil.

Many of the people of Ghana and other West African countries are from families who have been farmers for hundreds of years. Today's farmers cultivate much of the land using methods their ancestors developed. Some fields are still tilled with wood-handled iron hoes.

In earlier times, most African men handled the hunting and administrative matters of the home and village. African women were responsible for planting and harvesting the crops. Cooking and meals were scheduled around the women's work schedule. Meals were usually served twice a day, with a light snack in the evening. The morning meal was often eaten before 6:00 A.M. and usually consisted of a heavy porridge made from sorghum, corn, millet, or

This Ancient Egyptian art shows grapes being harvested.

rice. The porridge was flavored with milk, bits of meat, peppers, vegetables, or fruits. Adults also ate kola nuts, which are high in caffeine, to make them feel more alert. This practice is similar to people drinking coffee or soft drinks to get the same effect.

At the hottest part of the day, around noon, the women would return from the fields to eat and rest. The largest meal of the day was eaten during this time, when stews, soups, and fu fu would be served. Fu fu is made by pounding starchy grains or vegetables such as yams, cocoyams, or millet into a flour and then boiling them to make a dough.

When the sun went down, the workday was over. A light snack of fruits, yam fritters—which are mashed, seasoned, and fried yams—or batter-covered bits of meat or fish called samosas made up the evening meal.

Today during the harvesttime, there are many areas in Africa where the grain is threshed by beating it with paddles as was done long ago. Women grind corn and millet into flour and meal by pounding the kernels with a wooden pestle in a hollow tree trunk. A specially high grade of millet is finely ground into a flour called teff. Teff flour makes a wonderful pancakelike bread called injera.

The use of wild yams for food may go back as far as when millet was first planted. African yams are thick, oblong tubers usually a little over a foot long. Tubers are plants that have short, thick, fleshy stems that grow underground. Yams and white potatoes are two of the many types of tubers. African yams come in many shapes, colors, and sizes. Some African Igname yams weigh as much as 100 pounds. When a yam is boiled, it tastes like a dry, mealy white potato.

In Africa, yams became such an important part of the diet that they were given almost mystical qualities. The yam was included in many ceremonies, from the celebration of a new birth to the memorial for the death of an elder. Elaborate festivals honoring the yam were created in Ghana and other West African countries. Harvest celebrations that recognize the yam are still held in Africa.

Traditionally, meat was not eaten or served in large quantities in Africa and was usually reserved for special celebrations. In many African dishes, small cubes

Women in modern Africa make flour from millet
in much the same way as their ancestors did.

A yam festival on the Ivory Coast of Africa

of meat were used as flavoring as part of stews or soups and served with a starch, like fu fu. Pinches of fu fu dough were used to scoop up the soup or stew.

Salt was hard to come by and was highly prized as a way of preserving food. Peppers, such as the melegueta and guinea pepper, and ginger were more abundant and were used to make the dishes spicy and flavorful.

Sesame seeds are another early food from Africa and were traded throughout the continent and the Eastern world starting around 2000 B.C. People used the seeds, which have a nutlike flavor, as a seasoning and as a cooking oil.

Pumpkins and calabashes are edible gourds that were native to the famous cities of Timbuktu and Gao on the Niger River in Africa. The dried gourds were made into dishes, spoons, and food storage vessels.

Fruits of many varieties grow on the African continent. Wild oranges and lemons were found in Senegambia as early as the mid-1400s by Portuguese

Dried gourds serve as utensils and storage containers.
They are often beautifully decorated.

travelers. Dates and figs have been available since before biblical times. The fruit of the tamarind, besides being made into a refreshing beverage called dakhar in modern Senegal, is also used medicinally as a mild laxative. Many types of melons, including watermelons, have been grown in Egypt for thousands of years. Wild watermelons are also native to a number of Africa's tropical regions.

Palm trees are found in most parts of Africa. The palm tree produces coconuts, dates, palm nuts, and palm oil, which is used as the basis for soups and stews as well as for making household products.

Africa is also the home of the legendary baobab tree, which produces a fruit that can be eaten and has a trunk that can grow as thick as 30 feet in diameter. The baobab tree is used to make rope, cloth, paper, and medicine. The nuts from the tree are ground into a flour used to thicken sauces. Large truffles, which are mushroomlike plants, grow on or near the roots of the trees. They are very tasty when peeled and cooked over coals or used in broths.

A large assortment of the fruits and vegetables that are eaten in the Americas and the Caribbean were brought there from Africa by explorers and missionaries. René Caillé, a Frenchman who traveled from Morocco to Guinea in 1830, had high praise for the meals he was served during his journey. In his journal, Caillé writes about a "luncheon of rice with chicken and milk," a type of couscous served with a sauce made of greens. Another Frenchman, Theophilus Conneau, wrote in 1827 that the "mutton minced with roasted ground nuts (peanuts) and rolled up into a shape of . . . meat balls, which when stewed up with milk, butter and a little malaguetta pepper is a rich dish. . . ."

When the slave trade began, millions of Africans were brought to North and South America and the Caribbean to work in the homes and fields of their masters. When the African captives were transported from their countries, several types of trees and plants from their region traveled with them as part of the cargo.

A number of foods used in African cooking became a part of cookery in the New World. For example, sesame was successfully grown in South Car-

The baobab tree of Africa is very useful. Its huge trunk may be hollowed out to store water, and it produces an edible fruit.

olina during the 1750s and is still called by its Wolof name "benne" in many parts of the South. Sesame wafers are a popular type of cracker in this area, and hamburger buns sprinkled with sesame seeds are served throughout the United States.

Other food plants Americans eat that are considered native to Africa are a variety of leafy greens such as spinach, black-eyed peas, chick peas (garbanzo beans), kidney beans, fava beans, and lentils. Africans ground some types of the beans into flour and made them into fritters. Eggplant, cucumbers, garlic, and onions came from central Africa. Okra is common throughout much of Africa and was first used as a thickener for various sauces and stews.

Thousands upon thousands of the captives died during the journey across the ocean. This journey, called the middle passage, was torture for the Africans. They had lost their freedom, their homes, and their families. They were forced to live in cramped, filthy quarters below deck, and they suffered from disease and poor nutrition.

Alexander Falconbridge was a surgeon on a slave ship in the mid- to late 1700s. In his book *An Account of the Slave Trade on the Coast of Africa,* he writes about a typical meal for the African captives:

> *The diet of the Negroes while on board, consists chiefly of horsebeans [fava beans] boiled to the consistence of a pulp; of boiled yams and rice and sometimes of a small quantity of beef or pork. They [the sailors] sometimes make use of a sauce composed of palm-oil mixed with flour, water and red peppers, which the sailors call slabber-sauce. Yams are the favorite food of the Eboe or Bight Negroes, and rice or corn of those from the Gold and Windward Coasts; each preferring the produce of their native soil.*

One reason many researchers believe that the West African captives were able to survive the middle passage and slavery was that they were accustomed to a vegetable-based diet.

Millions of Africans were taken to the islands of the Caribbean to provide labor for the sugarcane crops and the homes of European masters, and to produce the refined sugar that made their masters rich. The African captives combined the knowledge of their native plants and vegetables, the plants and vegetables from their new homes, and a blend of African, Indian, and European cooking techniques to develop a new Afro-Caribbean cuisine.

AFRO-CARIBBEAN COOKING

Many varieties of food found in the Caribbean owe much to the native Amerindians who lived there hundreds of years before Columbus arrived. The Arawaks grew cassava, which is also common in African countries. Cassava is the white starchy root of the manioc plant. When cooked, it turns mushy and has a bland taste. Tapioca is made from the cassava root and is used to thicken sauces and puddings. The juice of the cassava was used to make a potent, fermented alcoholic drink and, when mixed with salt and pepper, to make a seasoning for meats called cassareep. The Arawaks also invented a food preservative from the cassava.

Garlic, corn, and many of the fruits associated with the West Indies such as papaya, guava, pineapples, and mamey (an apricotlike fruit) were also grown. The Arawaks ground up berries with the leaves of selected trees and plants to make special spices. A savory meat and hot-pepper stew called pepperpot, which is still very popular in the Caribbean, is also of Arawak origin.

The Arawaks cooked foods over aromatic wood fires, making them one of the earliest people in the Americas to barbecue. The word *barbecue* came from the Spanish word *barbacoa*, which in turn was taken from the vocabulary of the Arawak Taino people that once lived in Haiti.

Most of the Arawaks died in battles with fierce warrior peoples like the Caribs (for whom the Caribbean is named today) and from diseases brought to the islands by the Spanish Conquistadors. The Arawaks that were left were subjected to the brutality of the Spanish, who overpowered the natives as they colonized the islands of the Caribbean.

In the seventeenth century the Spanish brought people from West Africa to the islands to work as slaves on the vast sugar plantations. Many modern Afro-Caribbeans can trace their lineage directly to specific peoples in Africa. Most Haitians have ancestors that lived in the West African country of Dahomey (now called Benin). Slave ships from there brought pigeon peas.

Upon reaching Jamaica in 1687, Sir Hans Sloan observed that peanuts—called earthnuts by the sailors—"brought from Guinea in the Negroes Ships" as well as sesame, okra, and "white Pease with a black Eye [black-eyed peas]"

An early engraving of slaves cultivating sugarcane in the West Indies

were growing on the island. Okra was already being "very carefully planted by Europeans, as well as Slaves."

In 1792 British Navy Captain William Bligh brought Tahitian breadfruit to the Caribbean from Tahiti, an island in the South Pacific Ocean. It was intended to be a cheap, starchy food for the slaves who worked on the English sugar plantations. At first, the slaves refused to eat the breadfruit because of its musky smell and doughlike texture, and they fed it to the animals. When the slaves began cooking the breadfruit on small grills or in coal pots, it became a popular food.

Captain Bligh is also credited with bringing the ackee tree to the West Indies. When this fruit is on the tree, its appealing red color invites you to take a bite—but beware! The ackee fruit is not ripe and is deadly poisonous until it has burst open to reveal the yellow edible portion inside. Slave cooks knew how to prepare ackee, and their delicious recipes have made this one of the most popular dishes in Jamaica.

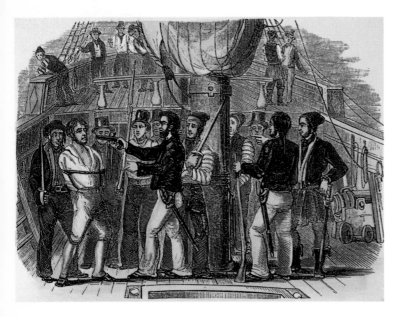

In 1789 mutineers forced Captain Bligh of the HMS Bounty *and 18 members of his crew into a 23-foot boat. They sailed 3,900 miles in the small boat to Indonesia. Captain Bligh resumed his career in the British navy in 1791 and later introduced Tahitian breadfruit to the Caribbean.*

Africans enslaved in the Caribbean used okra, yams, and various types of beans and greens in much the same way they had before, but other African dishes changed slightly in the Caribbean. Fu fu became known there as coocoo and was made out of cornmeal. The African dishes of kenkey and dokono, which were small portions of mashed plantain or grated corn wrapped in banana leaves and steamed until cooked, came to be known as conkies in Jamaica. Fish and shellfish abound in the Caribbean, and Africans who lived in coastal areas were familiar with preparing seafood in a variety of ways. Many of the recipes created by the African slave cooks became so popular that they are still prepared today.

The term *Creole* is often used to describe the dishes from the Caribbean that were created by Amerindians and African slaves, but they were not the

Fish are an important part of the diet in the Caribbean.
This catch in Jamaica may be prepared in a variety of ways.

only people to influence the art of cooking in the area. *Creole* actually means "people born in the West Indies of European descent." The Caribbean islands were dominated by the French, Dutch, English, and Spanish. The mixture of Amerindian, African, and European cuisines is what makes Caribbean recipes so unique and delicious.

The Spanish brought cabbage, onions, and sugarcane to the islands. They also brought the sweet oranges from Seville in Spain. The Spanish are also given credit for the islands' lime and banana trees. The French introduced the use of chives, along with sophisticated cooking methods such as poaching fish in peppers with spices. All the Europeans including the English brought their taste for salted codfish. Africans who worked as slave cooks combined the recipes they learned from their European masters with their own cooking techniques. Many dishes did not change that much from island to island except that they were called by different names, according to which European government controlled the area.

Hot peppers also played an important part in the history of Afro-Caribbean cooking. The Arawak Amerindians created a hot-pepper marinade called jerk, which was used on meat before barbecuing. Jerk was later used by runaway slaves called Maroons to preserve their food in the hot and humid climate of Jamaica. The Maroons in hiding were able to survive on jerk meat while they used guerilla tactics to fight against their European slaveholders. Eventually, they won their freedom. Originally, barbecuing was done in pits with hot charcoal placed over the meat. Later it developed into a popular island tradition.

In the Brazilian markets, slave women sold delicious dishes, many of which retained their African names and flavors. Abara, for example, is a spicy bean dish flavored with palm oil and peppers. Acaraje is a deep-fried black-eyed pea fritter made by grinding the peas into a paste, seasoning them with peppers, and filling them with dried smoked shrimp. Coconut and rice confections sweetened with honey or cane sugar are also popular. African cooks influenced Brazil's cuisine to produce dishes reflecting the best of both worlds.

The meals of the rich European plantation owners in the Caribbean became legendary. A typical 10:00 A.M. breakfast in 1772 was described as including bacon, ham, beef, fowl, broiled pigeons, plantains, roasted sweet cassavas, bread, butter, and cheese, all of which were washed down with glasses of beer and wine. Dinner, which was served around 3:00 P.M., included more of the same, along with vegetables, breads, coffee, and rich desserts.

The slaves on these sugarcane plantations did not share in the lavish meals of their masters. Manioc flour, cassavas, and salt beef or fish were rationed out to the slaves. Some slave owners were so cruel that they provided only rum for the slaves as it was cheaper and enabled the intoxicated slaves to work with very little nourishment. Slave gardens were encouraged in the British colonies, and the vegetables the slaves grew were added to their rations. Herbs and grasses were brewed into teas, and sugarcane was used as a sweetener for simple desserts and candies. The slaves learned to "make do" with what little they had and still prepared tasty meals.

Although African influences spread throughout the Caribbean, it is not easy to trace them in detail. Africans had their own food preparation and cooking methods. Anthropologist William Bascom, who studied the Yoruba people of southwestern Nigeria and Africans in other regions of West Africa, found that there are six basic ways Africans cooked their food: boiling in water, steaming in leaves, frying in deep oil, toasting beside the fire, roasting in the fire, and baking in ashes. The heavy skillets, three-legged pots called spiders, tightly

The three-legged pot is used throughout Africa and the Caribbean to cook many different dishes.

woven baskets, pottery, calabashes, and gourds that cooks used in Africa continue to be used in the Caribbean and the Americas.

It became a trend in America to purchase Africans who had been enslaved, or "seasoned" as it was called, in the Caribbean for a period of time. As the Africans traveled from the Caribbean to America, their recipes and methods of cooking moved with them. The African cooks introduced recipes and techniques that have become an important part of American cuisine, such as the uses of peppers and the preparation of greens, rice, and beans. The creative genius of these slave cooks changed the way foods were seasoned and prepared in colonial America.

THREE

THE IMPACT OF SLAVERY

Slavery grew slowly at first in colonial America, and as it spread, it brought about a new American social and political order. New laws, customs, and rules were created around the slave trade. The humanity of the African captives was often disregarded in order to make the colonists rich. Slaves were forced to work in the fields and homes of white Americans from dawn to dusk.

Africans from the rice-growing regions of West Africa were bought to work in the rice fields of South Carolina and Georgia. Rice from Madagascar, an island off the coast of East Africa, was first grown by African slaves in South Carolina. Over hundreds of years they had developed expert techniques for planting and harvesting rice. The early efforts of African slaves transformed the production of rice into a major agricultural industry.

As much as possible, the African captives tried to hold on to their traditional beliefs and culture while adapting to their new life in a strange place. However, many African cultural traditions became blended with the way of life in the Americas.

The captives were also greatly influenced by Native Americans. Many

African Americans believed that they had much in common with the American Indians. Like the American Indians, Africans had a long tradition of developing ways to survive from the plants and animals of the land. Indians often taught African slaves how to hunt animals and prepare them for cooking with Native American plant foods. African Americans learned how to grind the leaves of the sassafras tree into a powder to make file. File was used to thicken soups and stews.

The northeastern tribes of the Iroquois and Powhatan shared their methods of preparing fish, wild game, beans, corn, and squash with African Americans. The Narragansett and Penobscot tribes showed African Americans how to make corn pudding and succotash, and how to use the pumpkin in different ways. Plains Indians such as the Cheyenne, Crow, and Dakota taught them how to preserve meat and fish by drying it to make jerky.

Africans were accustomed to their food being very hot and spicy. The southwestern Hopi, Pueblo, Apache, and Navajo all knew how to use different chili peppers to flavor their food. They also ate fry bread and showed African Americans how to make it. And Indians introduced them to different kinds of American melons.

American Indian recipes were adapted and later brought to the South by African-American cooks. Slave cooks combined the methods used by Native Americans and Europeans with cooking techniques of their own to create a unique new African-American cuisine. The slave owners soon realized that the African cooks had a special talent for preparing tasty dishes. In the late 1600s, many colonial women had their slave cooks and their helpers prepare the meals and take care of the cleaning. This practice was as common in the North as it was in the South, although slavery in the northern colonies was less widespread.

The southern plantation kitchen was the slave cooks' domain, and they reigned supreme. An unhappy cook had many deadly ways of executing vengeance, which may be why they received a little more consideration from the white household than other slaves. Frederick Law Olmsted, who wrote a book about his travels through the South in the 1800s, noted that the mis-

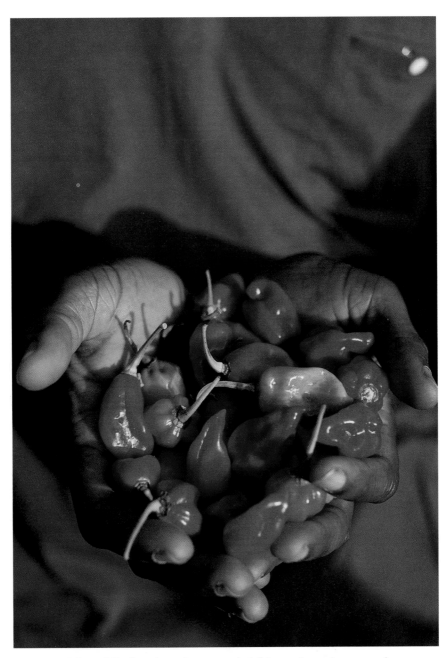

*Many Native Americans and African Americans used
chili peppers to add a special flavor to their cooking.*

tresses of the plantations he visited seemed to know very little about cooking and were happy to leave the operation of the kitchen in the hands of their cooks. On some plantations, the cook was also responsible for planning the meals and procuring the food.

Wealthy women sometimes prepared food, but only for grand balls or special occasions. Their cooking was usually limited to various pastries such as pies or cakes. Although elaborate meals were prepared by slave cooks for the colonial families, this food was not shared with the slaves.

Noted author Frederick Douglass was a former slave. He has left a detailed account of the kind of meals slave owners often consumed:

> *The close-fisted stinginess that fed the poor slave on coarse cornmeal and tainted meat . . . wholly vanished on approaching the sacred precincts of the Great House itself. . . . Immense wealth and its lavish expenditures filled the Great House with all that could please the eye or tempt the taste. Fish, flesh, and fowl, were here in profusion. Chickens of all breeds, ducks of all kinds . . . guinea fowls, turkeys, geese, and peafowls (pheasants) . . . partridges, quails, pigeons. . . . Beef, veal, mutton, venison. . . . The teeming riches of the Chesapeake Bay, its rock perch, drums, crocus, trout, oysters, crabs, and terrapin, were drawn here to adorn the glittering table. . . . Here were gathered figs, raisins, almonds, and grapes from Spain, wines and brandies from France, teas of various flavors from China, and rich, aromatic coffee from Java, all conspiring to swell the tide of high life, where pride and indolence lounged in magnificence and satiety.*

Slaves were required to spend most of their time working on the plantation's cash crop. Once they began working in the field, they were usually not allowed to go back to their cabins to prepare something to eat. Hoecakes were made by many slaves as a way to get a quick, hot meal during the short break allowed at noontime. The hoecake recipe below is from a slave narrative. It is easy to see why they called them "hoecakes":

Stand in the shade near the edge of the field. Light a fire from whatever brush and twigs there may be. On the greased side of the blade of your hoe, mix meal and water until it is thick enough to fry. Add salt if you remembered to bring any. Lean the hoe into the fire until the top side of the bread bubbles. Flip it and brown the other side. If you do it without a hoe, you have to make suitable changes in the kitchen.

The few opportunities that slaves had for time off were used to go hunting and fishing. Possum became a popular game food because it was a night creature that could be hunted when the slaves were not working. They also trapped animals such as rabbits, squirrels, and raccoons. Slaves that lived near a river or stream could go fishing and add various kinds of fish to their meager diet. The few slaves that got chickens usually raised them to produce their own eggs and as an occasional source of meat. From time to time, some slaves were also supplied with coffee, molasses, or salt.

In the cooler months, slave cooks prepared meals in their crude cabin fireplaces. Everything from cornbread to cakes was baked in the fireplace in a Dutch oven, which was a large cast iron pot with a tight-fitting lid. During the heat of the summer, meals were often prepared outdoors, as they had been in Africa.

Some plantations had large communal kitchens and dining areas where everyone in the slave quarters prepared and ate their meals. On one plantation in Texas the wake-up call was sounded at 4:00 A.M. Breakfast was usually bread, molasses, coffee, and sometimes a pickled herring or a piece of mackerel. Charles Ball, a freed slave who wrote the book *Fifty Years in Chains,* stated that the slaves on his plantation received "cornbread that had been baked in ashes and . . . water for us to drink. . . . An old woman, who was not capable of doing much work in the field . . . baked the bread for the whole gang."

Food for the children was usually placed in a trough, similar to those used

*This painting of a slave cabin shows that
cooking was often done outdoors over a log fire.*

by pigs, and was eaten with their hands. A typical meal was cornbread soaked with "pot likker," which is the liquid that is left over from cooking vegetables.

Many slaves resisted eating in a communal kitchen because it took away what little privacy and family life they had. One slave owner wrote that he preferred a common kitchen for his slaves but "those among them who have families prefer to serve their food for themselves in their own peculiar way."

On some plantations, slaves were provided with land for communal gardens or small individual plots of land where they could plant whatever they liked. But slaves had very little free time to tend the gardens, which might be far from where they lived. Often the slaves could not grow enough produce for them to become self-sufficient.

From the viewpoint of the slaveholder, the purpose of having slaves was to get as much labor from them as was possible without spending much money. In other words, the food that the slaves were given to eat was considered feed, such as what you would give livestock.

Frederick Douglass wrote that

> . . . *slaves on Col. Lloyd's farm received, as their monthly allowance of food, eight lbs. of pickled pork, or its equivalent in fish. The pork was often tainted, and the fish were of the poorest quality. With their pork or fish, they had given them one bushel of Indian meal, unbolted, of which quite fifteen per cent was more fit for pigs, than for men. With this, one pint of salt was given, and this was the entire monthly allowance for a full-grown slave, working constantly in the open field from morning till night every day in the month except Sunday.*

In the course of his research on slavery, historian John Hope Franklin found that "food was, on the whole, insufficient for slaves. . . . slaves were generally ill fed. On one plantation each adult slave was given a pint of grain and half a herring (not infrequently rotten) for twenty four hours. . . . no plantation was found where a slave received more than nine pints of corn and one lb. of salt meat per week."

Starches, fats, and a few fruits and vegetables made up the meals of most slaves. Those who lived in Georgia and South Carolina ate cracked rice with salt pork, fish, wild game, or vegetables as the main part of their diet. A popular dish in the South was called Hoppin' John. It was a combination of rice and black-eyed peas and was similar to a dish prepared in Africa.

Most of the meat that the slaves were given consisted of the worst parts of the cow, chicken, and pig. Tripe, which is the stomach lining of a cow, and the intestines and stomach lining of a pig known as chitterlings and hog maws were considered slave food. Often, all the slaves had for meat rations were pork skins. The slaves cooked the skin in a skillet until it "crackled," hence the name for the delicious bits of skin and crispy meat that remained after the fat had been rendered. Slave cooks mixed the "cracklings" in their cornbread batter or cooked them with vegetables.

The slave cooks adapted many time-honored recipes from their African homelands by substituting ingredients. Cornmeal was used to make couscous, a North African dish. Couscous was made by boiling water, milk, and cornmeal until the mixture was thick. African yams were unavailable in America so slaves used sweet potatoes as a substitute. They called the sweet potatoes yams because they had a shape similar to African yams. Some sweet potatoes even had white flesh like a yam, although they tasted different.

Potatoes and corn were cooked in the ashes of a fire, often wrapped in cabbage leaves, similar to the way banana leaves were used in Africa. A type of coffee was made out of roasted okra, corn, or other grains and might be sweetened with molasses, if there was any available. Sassafras bark was boiled to make tea. It required a highly skilled cook to season and prepare the rations the slaves were given so that the food was edible. Due to the slave cooks' ability to adapt and invent recipes, many tasty new dishes were created that are still popular today.

The influence of the African slave cook upon the American diet became more and more evident as the first cookbooks appeared at the end of the eighteenth century. *The Virginia House-Wife* by Mary Randolph was one of the first cookbooks tailored to the American way of cooking. Published in 1824, it included three dishes containing okra, as well as a recipe for peanuts. Sarah Rutledge's cookbook *The Carolina Housewife,* which was published in 1847, used "bennie," or sesame seeds as they are most commonly known, as well as "groundnuts" in her candy recipes. And she was one of the first cookbook authors to include a recipe for "Hoppin' John."

The origin of the recipes in these cookbooks was never mentioned, but the use of peppers, rice, black-eyed peas, peanuts, and okra as ingredients indicated the recipes came from inventive African-American chefs.

FOUR

CREOLE, FRENCH, AND CAJUN COOKING

In many studies of the history of food in the Western World, the major emphasis has been on European-based dishes and recipes. Often, the contributions made by African-American cooks are not mentioned. However, although their innovative genius has often gone unrecognized, African-American chefs have made an impact on America's tastebuds.

The influence of African-American slave cooks was evident in the southern states, but especially in Louisiana. The Creole cuisine that started in the Caribbean continued to develop and evolve in New Orleans. The French fled Saint Domingue (which became Haiti after the slave revolts) and moved to New Orleans with all of their household slaves. It wasn't long before slave cooks introduced Creole food to America.

Louisiana has been described as "the most food-conscious and cuisine-rich state in the nation" by writer John Egerton. Egerton says that Louisiana ". . . has given us two of the most distinctive cooking styles to be found anywhere in the world. New Orleans-born Creole and bayou-born Acadian (Cajun) are like city and country cousins, the one rich and elegant and sophis-

ticated, the other earthy, spicy, straightforward—and both of them confi-
dently, even arrogantly, superior."

The upper-class French first brought recipes to Louisiana that had been
borrowed from other Old World countries. When Spain took over Louisiana
in the late 1700s, the Spanish dined in French homes and married French
women. Soon the French and Spanish people began to enjoy each others'
food, which started a type of cooking that took on the characteristics of both
countries.

Cajun cooking began when French peasants were deported from the Nova
Scotia region of Canada after the French and Indian War. They settled in New
Orleans and brought their simple ways of cooking to the French and Spanish
foods already present. Cajun cooking was born. The Cajun cooking style was
passed on to the African-American women servants or slaves, who usually were
the cooks.

Foods native to Africa were used in Creole cooking. Red pepper, rice, and
okra are popular ingredients. Gumbo Z' Herbes and Chicken Gumbo are
examples of some of the new foods created in America by African-American
cooks. The cooks would add many of these ingredients to the common colonial foods available, which would change them into greatly appealing dishes.

An example of the influence that African native foodways had upon local
New Orleans food is in the popular dish called jambalaya. Jambalaya is a highly
seasoned rice dish that can include any combination of pork, beef, seafood, or
chicken. The jambalaya first introduced by the Spanish in the late sixteenth
century was prepared using only pieces of ham with rice. The slaves who
cooked it "Creole style" added shrimp, chicken, crab, and other ingredients to
make it a tastier dish.

There is a difference between the Cajun-Creole food of New Orleans and
the Creole dishes of the Caribbean islands. Caribbean Creole cooking has
more peppers, tomatoes, tomato paste, lard, tubers, fruit, and various spices
such as cinnamon, nutmeg, ginger, clove, and allspice. Caribbean Creole
recipes, unlike many New Orleans dishes, use much less butter, cream, celery,
and basil. The French gravylike mixture of oil or butter and flour called roux

A milk cart making a delivery to a restaurant in early New Orleans

is New Orleans Cajun-Creole based. As if this wasn't confusing enough, Cajun-Creole gumbo can be made without okra. This would be unthinkable in Creole Gumbo. The word *gombo,* which became *gumbo* in the Americas, means okra in some of the Bantu languages in Africa.

Gumbo, like many Creole foods, kept its African roots and main ingredients, and it has been served all over the United States. African-American slave cooks prepared dishes like gumbo and jambalaya in the plantation house as well as in the White house. James Hemings, who was a slave chef for President Thomas Jefferson, even managed to cook his way to freedom.

Thomas Jefferson, the third president of the United States, lived very comfortably at Monticello, his plantation in Virginia. He loved gardening and entertaining and kept detailed notes about food and plants in his journals. He noted in one of his journals about his slaves' use of sesame seed, or benne. Although it took Jefferson a long time to decide whether to spell it "beni, benni, bene, beny, or benney," he quickly made up his mind about the value of sesame seed and the oil it produces as a cash crop once he tried sesame oil on his salad. "This is among the most valuable acquisitions our country has ever made," he wrote early in 1808.

Sesame oil was important during Jefferson's time because the war between France and England had disrupted the olive oil trade. American olive oil importers began to look for a substitute. They discovered that they had to look no farther than the slave quarters for a good-quality oil. African slaves continued to use sesame oil in their cooking. The state of South Carolina even promised a gold medal to the one who produced the most sesame oil.

Jefferson consulted agriculture books and botanists about growing sesame. He also observed how his slaves baked sesame seeds in their bread and boiled them in their greens to "enrich their broth." Jefferson "determined to go into the culture of it for domestic use." He recommended growing sesame to his friends and began planting the seed on his plantation.

Jefferson had numerous slaves who were responsible for every task on his large estate. The task of cooking, always considered a major responsibility, was given to James Hemings. Hemings traveled with Jefferson when he was

A view of Monticello, Thomas Jefferson's plantation in Virginia

appointed minister to France, and while there he was sent to French cooking schools. Hemings creatively combined many of the techniques of French cooking with his African roots and American foods.

"Thomas Jefferson came home from France so Frenchified that he abjured his native victuals," said his political rival, Patrick Henry. Jefferson enjoyed French food and Hemings prepared macaroni and cheese, cornbread stuffing, waffles, and ice cream for Jefferson's guests. These were considered unusual dishes in America at that time. Hemings was also one of the first American cooks to use raisins, almonds, and vanilla. In 1793 Jefferson freed Hemings on the condition that he train someone else to cook at Monticello.

Throughout history, African Americans like Hemings became famous chefs and caterers, opened restaurants, and provided other hospitality services. Although most masters kept a large portion of their earnings, the slaves were often able to use the money they earned from their cooking expertise to buy their freedom.

FIVE

African-American Chefs

Although racial prejudice made owning and maintaining a business difficult, many free blacks, as well as slaves, managed to make a name for themselves in the food industry as cookbook authors, restaurant owners, caterers, and chefs.

Washington, D.C., residents enjoyed the cooking skills of a number of chefs. Paul Jennings was a slave chef and wrote about his life in the White House under President James Madison. Henry Orr was considered to be the most "experienced and fashionable" waiter in the city. He often acted as a party consultant to Washington society. Jesse Garner, Andrew Brady, and Jarret Butler were just a few of the African Americans who owned oyster houses, popular eating places in Washington during the 1800s. John Gray was highly regarded as a caterer and restaurant owner there. James Wormley owned and operated a hotel in Washington known for its delicious meals and famous political guests. Wormley is famous for the turtle recipe he prepared in England to the "Queen's taste."

Elsewhere, African-American slave cooks Polly Haine, Jean Martin, and Flora Calvil were well known in Philadelphia in the 1790s for their delicious gumbo. The French Market in New Orleans was lined with coffee stands owned by African-American women. Hot rice fritters called cala were sold door-to-door by African Americans. African-American men and women loaded with baskets of pralines (a sweet candy made of brown sugar), waffles, and pies filled the streets of New Orleans as soon as the sun came up. In other states, slaves sold many other products such as eggs, vegetables, buttermilk, and corn to earn money.

In 1827 a freeman named Robert Roberts wrote *The House Servant's Directory*, which was a guide for caterers and managers of large estates, as well as servants. Roberts's book included instructions for everything from preparing recipes to setting a table properly. In 1847 Tunis Campbell published a similar book that included entertaining tips and recipes called *The Hotel Keepers, Head Waiters, and Housekeeper's Guide*. He also created an efficient system for servants who waited on tables. Through the use of his "drill," waiters learned their tasks with the precision of soldiers.

After the Civil War in 1865, several of the newly freed slave cooks left their pots and pans simmering on the fire and deserted the kitchen to find a new way of life. This placed their former masters and mistresses in a quandary—and in the kitchen. In many parts of the South, whites who had formerly owned plantations were left in poverty and starvation by the war. The foods and recipes that were formerly only considered good enough for slaves became the diet of both blacks and whites. Grits, black-eyed peas, Hoppin' John, greens seasoned with fatback, peanuts, cornbread, and cornmeal mush became staples on many southern dinner tables.

The publication and popularity of cookbooks greatly increased when slavery ended. The introduction to the *Picayune Creole Cook Book*, which was published in 1885, laments:

> the passing of the faithful old negro cooks—the "mamies" [which forced] the ladies of the present day to . . . acquaint themselves thoroughly with the art of cooking . . . to assist them in this, to preserve to future generations the many excellent and matchless recipes of

our New Orleans cuisine, to gather these up from the lips of the old Creole negro cooks and the grand old housekeepers who still survive, ere they, too, pass away, and Creole cookery, with all its delightful combinations and possibilities, will have become a lost art. . . .

Sadly, the skill the slave cooks brought to their masters' kitchens was noted only after it came to an end. However, cooking as an art and a business became a new way of life for many modern African-American chefs.

This once-elegant plantation house was burned in the Civil War. After the war, former slave cooks left the plantations and went to other parts of the country, taking their knowledge of food preparation with them.

African Americans began to move west. Approximately 5,000 to 8,000 African-American Civil War veterans became cowboys, wranglers, cooks, and trail bosses because these were the most plentiful jobs for black men. They were hired to drive great herds of cattle from the West to the cattle markets in the North and the East.

The cowboy cooks carried their food supplies on a horse or a pack mule and cooked over an open fire. These men had to be skilled with a gun as well as a skillet. The cook traveled well in front of the herd and the other cowboys to keep the dust from the horses and cattle out of the supplies. This meant that if there was an attack, the cook wouldn't have anyone to help him defend himself. There are many stories about cooks who single-handedly warded off attacks by Native Americans.

When the chuck wagon was invented, cowboy cooks were able to prepare a wider variety of meals. A chuck wagon could carry all the cooking utensils and supplies, such as barrels of molasses, beans, sugar, coffee, bacon, salt pork, and a two-day supply of water. Canned tomatoes and peaches were also stored in the chuck wagon.

Several African-American cowboy cooks, such as Wash Adams and Big Sam, were famous for their skills. Adams was known for his cooking and his singing. Big Sam was especially noted for his barbecuing skills. Antelope ribs, buffalo steaks, and wild turkey were a few of his specialties. African-American cowboy cooks are credited with introducing slow-cooking African-style stews, biscuits, and cornbread to the old West.

As America became covered with railroad tracks, more and more African Americans began working as cooks and porters on trains. A survey taken in 1921 revealed that out of sixty-three railroads, fifty-one had African-American cooks.

William Jackson began working as a railroad cook in 1946 and later was promoted to the position of chef. "Everything was first class . . . and all fresh," Jackson said. "Many movie stars rode with us and we had to . . . prepare food to their liking. The kitchens on these dining cars weren't equipped with air conditioning, so it was very hot. We used coal- and wood-burning stoves and a charcoal broiler for the steaks and chops, and to broil the fish."

Many African-American cowboys moved to the West after the Civil War.
A number of them were skilled in cooking, as well as in riding and roping.

Today a small number of African-American chefs practice their skills in the hospitality industry. "Minorities make up only 13 percent of those employees in the hospitality industry," says Chef Jason Wallace, president and cofounder of the Alumni Chapter of the Black Culinarians. "That's a big gap. Blacks have been in the kitchen area, but they haven't often held the title of Executive Chef or General Manager," added Wallace. "Now we are starting to see Blacks getting those titles. We are trying to create an awareness of the industry. We would like to make black youth aware of the opportunities in this field."

*This 1937 kitchen in the dining car was the most modern
of its time. It was part of an eight-car luxury train.*

African-American chefs are known for their innovative recipes, excellent restaurants, and superior culinary skills. For example, chef Edna Lewis, the descendant of freed slaves, has been committed to creating recipes, cooking dishes with the freshest ingredients, and writing cookbooks about authentic Southern cuisine.

Wiley Bates has known that he wanted to be a chef since he was 10 years old. "It was something I knew I would do for the rest of my life," says Bates. "I knew I would never get bored. I have a passion for the industry." Bates's

Edna Lewis, an African-American chef and cookbook author, is famous for her authentic Southern dishes.

cooking style combines a creative blend of East and West African, French, and Italian cooking traditions.

Chef T. J. Robinson blends elements of African, Cajun, Creole, Caribbean, Spanish, French, and her grandmother's cooking into what she calls "Louisiana Fancy Fine." People from all over the world have eaten Robinson's cooking. "That was one of my goals when I started," says Robinson. "I wanted to share my blackness, my African-American culture, my dream, my family and my food with others."

African-American chefs face the same struggles as African Americans in other areas of the business world. Chef Jacqueline Frazer says:

> *We have to work harder; we have to work longer, and we have to work for less. A chef once told me I had three strikes against me—I was a woman, I was Black and I was young. But I'm a strong believer that with hard work, with determination and a focused mind, you can do anything. The reason I'm where I am is due to this business being my whole life. I eat, sleep, walk, and talk food.*

In spite of everything, African-American chefs continue the tradition of culinary excellence that began with their African ancestors.

SIX

CONTRIBUTIONS TO AGRICULTURE

If it were not for the many contributions of African Americans to food production and agriculture, the United States could not have become the major food-producing nation that it is today. African Americans are responsible for numerous inventions and discoveries, although they have not always been given credit for their efforts.

African cultural traditions are deeply rooted in an appreciation and understanding of ways to get the land to be fruitful so that all people may eat well and be prosperous. The Europeans forcibly brought Africans to the Americas to do the work that was necessary for the crops to be successful. The Africans had many other talents that proved to be more valuable than their physical labor.

From the time of slavery to the great migration of African Americans from the South to the northern cities, many blacks worked as farm laborers. They began to develop tools and machines that could make their grueling tasks easier. Every new idea that made the work easier also had the dual benefit of increasing agricultural productivity.

After Emancipation, a former slave became one of the most famous African-American agricultural scientists in the world. In 1896 George Washington Carver began teaching at the Tuskegee Institute in Alabama, where he conducted thousands of experiments. It was through his tireless research that the South was liberated from its dependence on cotton as a cash crop. Because cotton had been planted for so many years, the soil was exhausted and the harvest was poor. Carver conducted an experiment with 20 acres of land that had poor soil. He planted black-eyed peas, which returned essential nutrients, such as nitrogen, to the soil, and the soil became fertile again. This experiment showed farmers how to rotate crops to keep the soil productive.

Carver became a world-famous expert on soil improvement, which allowed the planting and harvesting of a greater variety of food crops. He is best known for his development of hundreds of useful products from the peanut.

George Washington Carver (1864–1943) is shown here (second from right) teaching in a chemistry laboratory at Tuskegee Institute in Alabama in 1906. He received national acclaim for his research on peanuts. Among his many awards was the 1939 Theodore Roosevelt Medal for his valuable contributions to science.

He was also responsible for creating products from pecans, soybeans, and sweet potatoes. The demand for the products from these plants became so great that it created a new industry for the southern states. Carver developed over 350 products using plants grown in the South. Probably more than any other person, Carver was responsible for helping to lift the South from its devastated condition after the Civil War. He has been known as the "Farmers' Scientist" and has also been called the "Plant Doctor."

Carver wrote and published many bulletins that showed farmers and others how to better use common farm products. The bulletins covered everything from how to prepare the soil for planting to suggestions on how to prepare certain foods. His bulletin number 31, for example, was called "How to Grow the Peanut and 105 Ways of Preparing It for Human Consumption."

Carver was just one of many African Americans who made major contributions to agriculture and the food industry. For example:

- Norbert Rillieux was a native of New Orleans, born in 1806 to a white father and a mulatto (half white, half black) mother. His father was an engineer and a wealthy French planter who sent his son to some of the best Catholic schools in New Orleans and then to Paris to be educated. Because Rillieux was one-quarter African American he faced many forms of racial prejudice and discrimination, despite the fact that he had been trained in some of the best schools in engineering. In 1845 Rillieux made a major improvement to the sugar refining process that revolutionized the entire sugar industry.

- Henry Blair, an African American from Maryland, was able to get a patent for his corn seed planter in 1834. This invention made it much easier and faster to plant corn.

- John Stanard developed one of the earliest successful versions of the modern refrigerator. Stanard improved the old iceboxes by placing holes in special areas to help the air circulate. This helped to keep foods fresher for longer periods. He also had the idea of making different compartments for the icebox for different kinds of food. His patent was filed in 1891.

- R. P. Scott developed a device called a corn-silker that eliminated separating corn silk from the cob by hand. His machine, patented in 1894, made the process faster and more efficient.

- Joseph Lee made it easier for people to bake bread. Dough that used to have to be mixed by hand could now be mixed with Lee's bread kneading machine. He received a patent on his invention in 1894.

- F. J. Wood patented a machine in 1895 that made it much easier and faster to harvest potatoes. Wood's potato digger dug into the ground and loosened the dirt, which made it easier to pull up the potatoes.

Lloyd Augustus Hall (right) was chief chemist for Griffith Laboratories in Chicago, where he developed a number of processes important to the food industry.

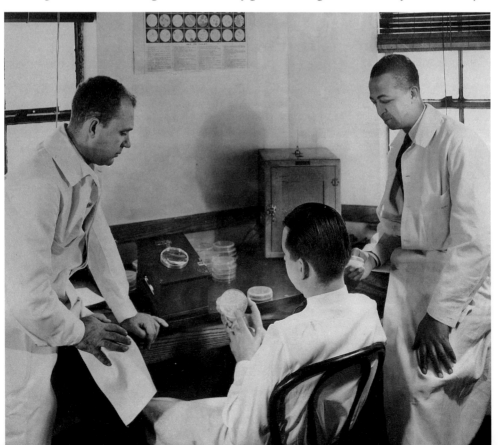

- J. T. White made a lemon-squeezing device that he patented in 1896. This was the first juicer that made it easy to squeeze the juice out of a lemon without the seeds and pulp.

- Lloyd Augustus Hall, as the chief chemist for Griffith Laboratories in Chicago, discovered how to make curing salts to preserve and process meats. His discovery completely transformed the meat packing industry. Over 25 patents are registered in his name for different processes used in the manufacture and packing of many food products, especially meat and baked goods. Born in 1894, Hall had a long and illustrious career.

- Frederick McKinley Jones was the inventor of the first refrigeration system for long-haul trucks. In the late 1930s he designed portable air-cooling units for trucks that would preserve perishable foods transported to markets from coast to coast. He became vice president of the U.S. Thermo Control Company, which made refrigeration units for trains, ships, and airplanes. Jones was considered an expert in refrigeration engineering and held over 60 patents. Forty of those were for refrigeration equipment. It was Jones's new inventions in refrigeration that completely changed the food transport industry and helped to create the international market for American food crops.

SEVEN

The Art of Modern Cooking

The availability in Africa of a variety of fresh fruits, grains, and vegetables is due to some of the richest soil on earth combined with a steady stream of tropical rainfall. Much of the land is ideal for raising cattle, sheep, pigs, and chickens. However, in certain parts of Africa, food is sometimes scarce. Both East African and West African cooks have developed an ability to create dishes out of whatever ingredients they have at the time. If an ingredient is not available, another may be substituted, or it can be left out entirely. Preparing dishes that use native ingredients and that are simple, delicious, and functional is a trait of African cooking. The meals for the most part are generally very spicy.

The basic African diet has not changed much over time. For the majority of the population, the meal is made up of a thick stew or soup that usually contains different vegetables and perhaps a little meat, poultry, or fish. A starch such as rice, bread, or fu fu is eaten with it. Yams may also be sliced into thin chips and fried. Other foods Africans enjoy are cocoyams, which are usually about the size of an American sweet potato, and plantains. Plantains look like large green bananas. They are not as soft or sweet as ripe yellow bananas

A woman in modern Zimbabwe cooking a simple midday meal

but they taste good when sliced and cooked over hot coals or fried in palm oil. Millet is a basic food of North Africa, where it is mixed with water and cooked to make a mushy porridge.

Europeans introduced tomatoes, corn, and chilies to Africans. It did not take long for these foods to become part of the African diet. Tomatoes are used in Senegal's tiebou dienn dishes. Bebere, an essential part of Ethiopia's doro wat (chicken stew), contains large amounts of dried chilies.

Sometimes African cooks prepare a one-pot meal that combines meat and starch, such as West African jollof rice. Diners break off a piece of bread or dip up a small amount of fu fu with the fingers to use as a scoop for the food on their plate.

An African family enjoys a meal. Traditionally, it is eaten without utensils.

Injera is a common and popular bread in Ethiopia and is an integral part of the meal. The main dishes are mounded in the center of several injera "pancakes," which are arranged on a serving platter so that they overlap each other and the edges hang over the rim. The platter is placed in the center of the mesob, a handmade wicker table shaped like an hourglass. The diners are seated on low couches or pillows. No forks, spoons, or knives are used. The right hand is washed thoroughly and, according to tradition, is the only hand permitted to be used throughout the meal. Each person breaks off a piece of the edge of the injera and uses it to scoop up a mouthful of food.

Africans usually eat a large meal only twice a day—at noon and in the evening—but they eat small snacks throughout the day. Fried plantains or meat on a stick, a piece of bread, or fresh fruit are the usual snacks. In African cities, street vendors sell them in open-air markets. Sweet snacks such as those commonly found in America are seldom eaten in Africa.

A typical snack in Africa is meat on a stick. Here, a Nigerian vendor keeps the snacks warm around a fire.

Outside the cities, the people in the countryside grow all their own fruits and vegetables in small gardens. Poultry, fish, and meat are less available and more expensive in the markets than fruits and vegetables, which is one reason soups and stews are a regular part of the diet.

It is still common in Africa for meals to have little or no meat in them at all. The amount of meat in a meal often depends on where a person lives. Where fish is cheaper than meat, such as in river or coastal areas, fish and meat are often combined into the same dish. Chicken is usually kept in reserve for guests or a special occasion. Sometimes meat, poultry, or fish is smoked or dried to preserve it, but most of the time it is served fresh.

Even in modern times most African cooks do not follow a recipe. Traditionally it was considered insulting to have to write down recipes. Cooking techniques and recipes are, for the most part, handed down orally from generation to generation. Also, an important part of African social life is centered around the preparation and serving of good, wholesome food. The cooking pots and pans that produce such an exotic array of dishes are as necessary a part of the culture as the music coming from the sound of festive drums.

An important part of the African-American experience is the way that Africans introduced many aspects of their food culture to America. This influence goes far beyond the chitterlings, grits, greens, cornbread, and hog maws that both blacks and whites describe as "soul food."

African-American cooking is usually associated with the history and culture of the South. Soul food has been a significant part of the black experience in America, but it is a separate and small part of the vast array of foods that make up African-American cooking. Soul food came about as a result of the economic condition and scarce resources of people that were considered to be poor.

There is an old saying in the South that says, "Rich folks who eat are just feedin' their body, but when poor folks eat they are feedin' their souls." The African slaves had few enjoyable times, but there was a good feeling that came when the slaves were able to fill their stomachs with humble but tasty meals. This raised the simple pleasure of eating to a higher level with religious observances, singing, or dancing. African-American cooks created soul food dishes to make eating as pleasurable a pastime as possible in spite of having to make do with whatever foods were available.

In American food culture, an abundance of beef and pork dishes in the diet was considered a sign of prosperity. Black slaves were given very little meat. They usually ate more fresh vegetables, poultry, cornmeal, fish, wild game, and those parts of the hog or cow that were thrown away by white people who could afford the better cuts of the meat. Soul food was like blues music in that it was created as a way for black people to cope with and survive their poor living conditions.

Modern African-American chefs have kept many of the traditional ways of cooking while modernizing others. Cooks and cookbook writers are adapting age-old recipes to make them healthier. These recipes retain the flavor of traditional southern soul food cooking but eliminate or use reduced amounts of salt, fat, and sugar.

Danella Carter's cookbook *Down Home Wholesome—300 Low-Fat Recipes from a New Soul Kitchen* seriously considers the important role that soul food has played in the survival of African Americans. Carter, like many cooks and dieticians today, strongly believes that the "survival food" of that time has outlived its usefulness. A lifelong diet of large amounts of soul food, much of it fried in oil, is now clearly a major factor in many of the sicknesses and ailments of African Americans today. Diets that are high in fat, salt, and sugar can lead to serious health problems, such as high blood pressure and cholesterol, diabetes, heart disease, and obesity. Substituting herbs and peppers for salt and sugar, and coconut, peanut, palm, and sesame oils for pork fats, chefs can keep traditional African-American dishes healthy as well as tasty.

Many African Americans are finding that the traditional African diet is generally healthier than what many Americans normally eat. For example, there are wonderful varieties of African food that do not require large amounts of oil to prepare and are naturally lower in fat and cholesterol. Also, modern nutritional experts believe that eating garlic regularly can help lower cholesterol levels, and West Africans use a lot of garlic in many of their dishes.

The art of African-American cooking is a celebration of African culture and tradition. Every time you eat okra gumbo, sesame seeds on a hamburger bun, a handful of peanuts, or black-eyed peas for good luck on New Year's Day, you are eating some of the foods that Africans introduced to the Western world. Further, African-American cooks have ingeniously adapted many traditional recipes to give them a unique flavor and appeal. They have become an important part of today's cuisine.

African and African-American Recipes

RULES TO REMEMBER

These recipes are fun and easy to prepare. There are, though, a few simple rules to remember before you begin to cook:

- Ask for adult permission and assistance when using any kitchen appliance, such as a microwave, blender, oven, mixer, can opener, etc.

- Remember, if you are using sharp utensils, be careful not to cut yourself or ask an adult to cut the items for you. Always cut in the direction away from your fingers and hands. Use a cutting board.

- If you are removing hot dishes from the stove top or oven, use oven mitts to protect your hands or ask an adult to remove the dish for you.

- If you are not sure about the measurements required in a recipe or if you do not understand the directions, ask an adult to help you.

- Always check to make sure you have all the ingredients listed in the recipe before you begin.

- Set out all the ingredients and utensils you need.

- Wash your hands before handling any food.

- Wash all fruits and vegetables you use to remove dirt.

- Chop, shred, or grate recipe ingredients first.

- Turn pot handles toward the back of the stove to prevent accidents.

- Be careful that oven mitts, dish towels, aprons, clothing, hair, ribbons, or other items on your person are not near an open flame.

ASHANTI PEANUT SOUP

Peanuts are called groundnuts in Africa. African captives introduced the peanut to American cooking. African-American scientist Dr. George Washington Carver experimented with the peanut to see if it could be grown as an alternative to cotton in the South. His research led to the development of more than 300 different products that could be made from peanuts. Dr. Carver used peanuts in everything from paint to peanut butter. Once, Dr. Carver invited several prominent people to dinner. After eating the delicious meal, his guests were amazed to learn that everything from the "meat" to dessert was made from peanuts! This recipe is a popular one in West Africa.

UTENSILS YOU WILL NEED

measuring cup and spoons, grater, knife, cutting board, small mixing bowl, heavy saucepan, long-handled mixing spoon, oven mitts, blender

INGREDIENTS

2 teaspoons flour	2 tablespoons grated onion
3 cups milk	¼ cup chopped parsley
3 cups canned chicken broth	½ teaspoon salt
2 cups crunchy peanut butter	½ teaspoon pepper

DIRECTIONS

Mix the flour and milk together in a bowl. Stir until the mixture is smooth. Pour the mixture into a heavy saucepan. Add the chicken broth, peanut butter, onion, parsley, salt, and pepper into a saucepan. Stir all the ingredients together. Turn the heat up high to bring the soup to a boil. As soon as the soup begins to boil, cut the heat down to low. Let the soup simmer for 15 minutes over low heat. Stir often.

When the soup has finished cooking, cover your hands with an oven mitt and carefully pour the soup into a blender. Blend for 3 minutes. If you do not have a blender, carefully stir the soup vigorously for 3 minutes. Pour the soup into individual bowls. Serve the soup while it is hot. Serves 6.

BAKED YAMS OR SWEET POTATOES WITH SPICED BUTTER

Yams are very popular in Africa. Many varieties of yams grow there. African yams are usually long and knobby and are white on the inside. African yams are also called cocoyams, wateryams, or white yams. Some Oriental and specialty markets carry African yams when they are in season. When the African captives arrived in America as slaves, the yams they were accustomed to did not grow here. They substituted American sweet potatoes in recipes that called for yams.

UTENSILS YOU WILL NEED

vegetable brush or dishtowel, measuring spoons, cookie sheet, small mixing bowl, mixing spoon, oven mitts

INGREDIENTS

6 large yams or sweet potatoes   1 tablespoon vegetable oil

Spiced Butter

4 tablespoons butter or   ¼ teaspoon cinnamon
   margarine, softened   ¼ teaspoon nutmeg
3 tablespoons brown sugar

DIRECTIONS

Preheat oven to 450°F. Scrub the yams with a vegetable brush or a clean, wet dishtowel to remove any dirt. Rinse yams well. Rub the oil on the skin of each yam. Place yams on a cookie sheet, with the small ends of the yams to the middle and the large ends to the outside. Bake yams for 30 minutes. Do not turn off oven. Cover your hands with oven mitts. Remove yams on the cookie sheet from oven and prick them with a fork to allow the steam to escape. Return yams to oven and continue cooking for another 30 minutes. Yams are done when they can be easily pierced with a fork. Serve hot yams along with a bowl of spiced butter. Serves 6.

To make spiced butter: Mix the soft butter or margarine, cinnamon, nutmeg, and brown sugar together in a small bowl. Slice yams down the center and serve with the spiced butter.

CRACKLING CORN BREAD

Slaves were often given the skin of pigs as food. They cooked the skin until it "crackled" and all the fat melted away. Cracklings are a delightful addition to corn bread and greens and are available in many stores around the United States.

UTENSILS YOU WILL NEED

measuring cup and spoons, sifter, large mixing bowl, wooden mixing spoon or plastic spatula, 8-inch-square cake pan, oven mitts

INGREDIENTS

2 cups yellow cornmeal	½ cup commercially prepared cracklings
1½ teaspoons baking powder	1 cup buttermilk
½ teaspoon baking soda	2 eggs, beaten
1½ teaspoons salt	2 tablespoons bacon or ham drippings

DIRECTIONS

Preheat oven to 400°F. Sift cornmeal, baking powder, baking soda, and salt together. Add the cracklings, eggs, and drippings. Spread batter in a greased 8-inch-square baking pan. Bake for 25 to 30 minutes. Serves 4 to 6.

LIBERIAN RICE BREAD

Liberia was originally settled by newly freed slaves in the 1800s. The name *Liberia* comes from the Latin word "liber," which means free. This is a popular recipe in that country and is considered a great delicacy.

UTENSILS YOU WILL NEED

measuring cup and spoons, mixer, large mixing bowl, wooden mixing spoon or plastic spatula, 8 x 12-inch rectangular or 9-inch round cake pan, oven mitts

INGREDIENTS

2 cups Cream of Rice cereal

4 tablespoons sugar

1 teaspoon baking soda

1 teaspoon salt

½ teaspoon nutmeg

3 cups mashed bananas

1 cup water

½ cup vegetable oil

DIRECTIONS

Preheat oven to 400°F. In a large mixing bowl, mix together by hand or with a mixer the Cream of Rice cereal, sugar, baking soda, salt, and nutmeg until well blended. Stir in the bananas, water, and vegetable oil. Stir until mixture is smooth, about 3 minutes. Spoon batter into 8 x 12-inch rectangular or 9-inch round cake pan. Bake for 30 minutes or until lightly browned. Cover your hands with oven mitts and remove bread from oven. Serve hot with butter or margarine. Serves 6.

UGANDAN SPINACH AND SESAME SEEDS

Sesame is called benne or simsim in many parts of Africa and the southern United States. African cooks use the tiny seeds in everything from main dishes to desserts.

Sesame seeds are very flavorful and are high in proteins, amino acids, calcium, and phosphorus. Sesame was introduced to the New World by African slaves.

UTENSILS YOU WILL NEED

measuring cup and spoons, heavy saucepan, spoon

INGREDIENTS

1 (10-ounce) package frozen
   chopped spinach, thawed
½ cup sesame seeds

3 to 4 tablespoons water
1 tablespoon butter

DIRECTIONS

Place water and sesame seeds in a heavy saucepan. Place the spinach in pan. Bring spinach to a boil, adding another tablespoon of water if necessary. Stir. Turn down heat and simmer until spinach is tender. Toss spinach with butter. Serves 4.

BLACK-EYED PEAS AND RICE (HOPPIN' JOHN)

Black-eyed peas were called cowpeas in Africa. The peas were transported from Africa to the West Indies and then into the Carolinas before the early 1700s. Eating black-eyed peas on New Year's Day is said to bring good luck in the new year.

UTENSILS YOU WILL NEED

measuring cup and spoons, knife, fork, 5-quart saucepan with a lid, spoon, oven mitt

INGREDIENTS

1 (10-ounce) package black-eyed peas

4½ cups water

¼ teaspoon salt

2 cups white rice, uncooked

1 small onion, diced

4 tablespoons margarine or butter

DIRECTIONS

Pour ½ cup of the water into a 5-quart pot. Place frozen black-eyed peas and salt in water. Turn heat to high. Cover the pot and bring it to a boil. Cover your hand with an oven mitt and remove the lid from the pot carefully so that the escaping steam does not burn you. Pour in the remaining 4 cups of water, the rice, onion, and margarine or butter. Stir. Cover the pot and return the contents to a boil. Turn the heat to low. Cook the black-eyed peas and rice for 20 minutes. Remove from the heat and let stand, covered, for 20 minutes. Remove the lid and stir the peas and rice with a fork. If the peas and rice are not tender and all the water is not absorbed, replace the lid and let the covered pot stand for another 5 minutes. Serve black-eyed peas and rice with Gambian Fish Caldou (recipe included in this section). Serves 6.

Okra with Corn

Okra is another vegetable that African captives introduced to the Western world.

UTENSILS YOU WILL NEED

measuring cup and spoons, knife, cutting board, heavy saucepan, spoon

INGREDIENTS

1 pound of fresh okra
  (small, even-sized pods) or
  1 pound frozen okra, sliced
1 medium onion, chopped

1 large tomato, chopped
1 cup frozen corn
⅛ teaspoon red pepper
1 teaspoon salt

DIRECTIONS

If using fresh okra, remove the tips and ends of the okra pods. Cut the okra into ½-inch slices. Place the okra, chopped onion and tomato, the corn, and the water in a saucepan. Stir the vegetables together. Turn the heat to medium and cook vegetables for 10 minutes, stirring occasionally. Mix in the red pepper and salt. Serve hot. Serves 6.

GAMBIAN FISH CALDOU

UTENSILS YOU WILL NEED

measuring cup and spoons, grater, knife, heavy skillet with a lid, spatula, platter, spoon

INGREDIENTS

6 fillets of mild fish (such as bass, catfish, cod, orange roughy, sole, trout, or flounder)

½ cup water

⅛ teaspoon red pepper

1 large onion, grated

1 bay leaf

1 teaspoon salt

DIRECTIONS

Gently rinse fish fillets under cold running water. Place the fish in a heavy skillet. Add the water, red pepper, grated onion, bay leaf, and salt. Turn up the heat to high. When the water starts to boil, turn the heat down to low. Cover the pan with the lid. Cook fish for 8 minutes. Fish is done when it is flaky but not mushy. The bay leaf is only used for seasoning and may be thrown away after the fish is done. Carefully remove fish from pan with a large spatula, and place the fish onto a platter. Slowly spoon the liquid remaining in the pan over the fish. Serve the fish while it is hot. Serves 6.

CARIBBEAN FRUIT PUNCH

UTENSILS YOU WILL NEED

measuring cup, long-handled spoon, large pitcher or punch bowl

INGREDIENTS

2½ cups lemonade

1 cup orange juice

1 cup pineapple juice

1 cup peach juice or nectar

DIRECTIONS

Mix all the juices together in a large pitcher or punch bowl. Serve punch over ice. Makes 6 eight-ounce cups, or 12 four-ounce cups.

NORTH AFRICAN ORANGE SALAD

UTENSILS YOU WILL NEED

knife, cutting board, measuring spoons, salad fork and spoon or two forks, small mixing bowl, and a salad bowl

INGREDIENTS

2 large oranges, sliced thin

2 cups lettuce, shredded

1 large onion, sliced thin

8 Greek olives, pitted and sliced

½ cup olive oil

4 tablespoons lemon juice

1 teaspoon salt

1 teaspoon pepper

DIRECTIONS

Using a salad fork and spoon, or two dinner forks, mix the lettuce, onions, and olives together in a salad bowl. Arrange orange slices on top. Mix oil, lemon juice, salt, and pepper together in a small bowl to make a salad dressing. Pour dressing over salad. Refrigerate. Serves 6.

Senegalese Cookies

These cookies are called *cinq centimes*, or "five-cent cookies," in the marketplaces of Dakar in Senegal. They are easy to prepare and are a great treat.

UTENSILS YOU WILL NEED

measuring cup, knife

INGREDIENTS

1 (16-ounce) package of
    sugar cookies

1 cup smooth peanut butter
1 cup chopped peanuts

DIRECTIONS

Spread each sugar cookie with peanut butter. Sprinkle chopped peanuts on top. Serves 6.

Homemade Peanut Butter

UTENSILS YOU WILL NEED

oven mitts, measuring cup, food processor, spatula, airtight container, large baking pan

INGREDIENTS

2 cups raw peanuts,
    shelled, skinned

1 to 1½ tablespoons peanut oil
½ teaspoon salt (optional)

DIRECTIONS

Preheat oven to 350°F. In a large, shallow baking pan, roast shelled nuts 15 to 20 minutes. Cover your hands with oven mitts. Remove pan from oven and cool. Put the peanuts, oil, and salt in a food processor with a metal blade. Pulse the machine to chop nuts coarsely until peanut butter has a smooth, creamy consistency—2 to 3 minutes. Scrape into jar or container with an airtight lid; store in refrigerator. If oil rises to the top of the container, stir it back in or pour it off before using peanut butter. Makes one cup of peanut butter.

Ghana Plantain Appetizer (Kelewele)

This West African appetizer tastes similar to American potato chips.

UTENSILS YOU WILL NEED

a knife, deep fryer or skillet, small bowl, measuring cup, teaspoon, slotted spoon, paper-towel-covered plate

INGREDIENTS

3 cups cooking oil

2 tablespoons water

1 teaspoon ground ginger

½ teaspoon salt

½ teaspoon ground red pepper

6 large unripened plantains,
   peeled and sliced ½ inch thick

DIRECTIONS

In a deep fryer or a skillet deep enough to cover the plantain slices, heat the oil until it is hot but not smoking. In a small bowl, combine the water, ginger, salt, and ground red pepper. Drop plantain slices into bowl one by one, coating each piece evenly. Carefully place the coated slices in the hot oil and deep-fry until golden brown, about 3 to 5 minutes. Remove the fried slices with a slotted spoon. Drain on paper towels. Yields 6 servings.

measuring cup and spoons, knife, cutting board, large pot or Dutch oven
with lid, large spoon

INGREDIENTS

3 cups water

2 cups chopped ham

1 tablespoon salt

1 dried cayenne pepper pod,
  to taste

½ teaspoon sugar

4 bunches collard greens

8 to 12 small okra pods, stemmed

DIRECTIONS

Place the water and the chopped ham in a heavy pot or Dutch oven. Add ½ tablespoon of the salt, the sugar, and the pepper pod to the ham. Simmer the ham
until it is tender and the fat dissolves, 15 to 20 minutes. Remove the pot from the
heat.

Cut the tough stems and yellow leaves from the greens and discard. Gently
rub the leaves with your fingers under warm running water. Cut the greens into
large pieces. Fill a sink or pan with warm water and add the remaining ½ tablespoon of salt. Let the leaves soak in the warm, salted water for 10 minutes. Rinse
with cool water and drain in a colander.

Add the clean greens to the pot with the ham. Return the pot to the heat and
cook over medium heat, stirring every 15 minutes until the greens are wilted but
not quite tender, for 30 to 45 minutes. Layer the okra on top of the greens. Cover
and continue cooking the greens for 20 minutes or until tender, stirring
frequently and adding hot water as needed to keep the greens from sticking.
Serves 6 to 8.

Baked Macaroni and Cheese

UTENSILS YOU WILL NEED

measuring cup and spoons, grater, saucepan, colander, small bowl, fork, ovenproof casserole dish

INGREDIENTS

6 cups water

1 tablespoon salt

2 cups elbow macaroni

¼ cup butter, plus 1 tablespoon softened

2 large eggs

2 cups evaporated milk

1 teaspoon salt

2 dashes Tabasco sauce, to taste

1 pound extra-sharp cheddar cheese, grated and mixed with ½ cup grated American cheese

½ teaspoon sweet paprika

DIRECTIONS

Preheat the oven to 350°F. Put the water and salt in a heavy saucepan and bring to a boil. Slowly stir in the macaroni. Boil for 12 minutes, stirring constantly. The macaroni should be firm but tender. Pour the macaroni into a colander and rinse with a little cold water. Drain as much water as possible from the macaroni. Mix the macaroni with the butter and set aside.

In a small bowl, beat the eggs with a fork until light yellow. Add the milk, the salt, and Tabasco sauce. Using the remaining tablespoon of butter, grease a 9-inch casserole dish. Alternate layers of the cooked macaroni with layers of the mixed cheeses, ending with the cheeses on top. Pour the egg mixture slowly and evenly over the macaroni and cheese. Sprinkle with the paprika. Bake for 30 to 40 minutes, until the egg custard topping is firm, bubbly, and golden brown.

GULLAH RICE

UTENSILS YOU WILL NEED

measuring cup and spoons, colander, saucepan with a lid

INGREDIENTS

1 cup uncooked rice	¼ cup shelled roasted red pistachios
2½ cups water	¼ cup minced celery
½ teaspoon salt	2 tablespoons margarine or butter

DIRECTIONS

Rinse the rice in a colander under cold running water. Drain. Put the water and salt in a medium saucepan. Add the rice, pistachios, celery, and margarine or butter and bring to a boil. Cover the saucepan and reduce the heat to low. Simmer for 15 minutes, until the rice is tender and the water is absorbed. Serves 2.

TANZANIAN BAKED BANANAS

UTENSILS YOU WILL NEED

measuring spoons, knife, cookie sheet or baking pan, oven mitts, small bowl, spoon

INGREDIENTS

4 large, ripe *unpeeled* bananas	3 tablespoons brown sugar
2 tablespoons melted butter	1 teaspoon freshly squeezed lemon juice

DIRECTIONS

Preheat oven to 425°F. Cut off the ends of the bananas. Place unpeeled bananas on ungreased cookie sheet or in baking pan. Bake for 15 minutes or until the skins burst and turn black. Peel and discard the skins and cut each banana lengthwise. Mix the butter, brown sugar, and lemon. Drizzle over the cooked bananas. Serves 8.

FURTHER READING

Carter, Danella. *Down Home Wholesome: 300 Low-Fat Recipes From a New Soul Kitchen* (New York: Dutton, 1995).

Hafner, Dorinda. *A Taste of Africa* (Berkeley, Cal.: Ten Speed Press, 1993).

Harris, Jessica B. *Iron Pots and Wooden Spoons: Africa's Gifts to New World Cooking* (New York: Atheneum (Macmillan), 1989).

Medearis, Angela Shelf. The African-American Kitchen: Cooking From Our Heritage (New York: Dutton, 1994).

Mullin, Sue. *Creole Cooking: The Taste of the Tropical Islands* (Secaucus, N.J.: Chartwell Books, 1993).

Osseo-Asare, Fran. *A Good Soup Attracts Chairs* (Gretna, Lou.: Pelican Publishing Company, 1993).

INDEX